Lee Bailey's
BERRIES

by Lee Bailey

Photographs by Tom Eckerle

CLARKSON POTTER/PUBLISHERS
NEW YORK

Published by Clarkson Potter/Publishers, 201 East 50th Street, New York,
New York 10022. Member of the Crown Publishing Group.

Random House, Inc. New York, Toronto, London, Sydney, Auckland

CLARKSON N. POTTER, POTTER, and colophon are trademarks of Clarkson
N. Potter, Inc.

Manufactured in China
Design by Howard Klein

Library of Congress Cataloging-in-Publication Data

Bailey, Lee.
    [Berries]
    Lee Bailey's berries / by Lee Bailey ; photographs by Tom Eckerle.
—1st ed.
        p.   cm.
    1. Cookery (Berries)   I. Title.
    TX813.B4B35   1994
    641.6'47—dc20   93-32752
                                                          CIP

ISBN 0-517-59237-1

10 9 8 7 6 5 4 3 2 1

First Edition

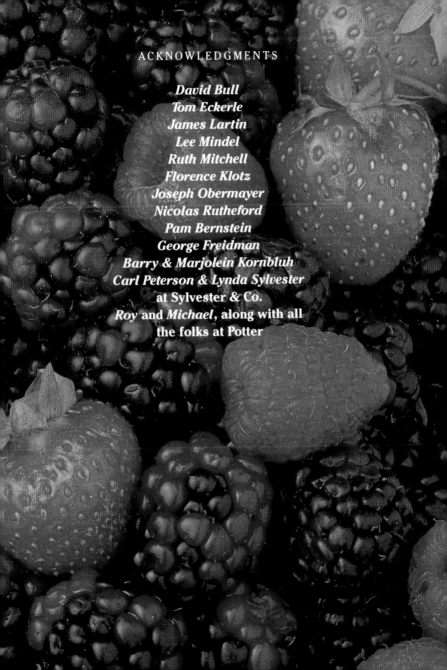

ACKNOWLEDGMENTS

David Bull
Tom Eckerle
James Lartin
Lee Mindel
Ruth Mitchell
Florence Klotz
Joseph Obermayer
Nicolas Rutheford
Pam Bernstein
George Freidman
Barry & Marjolein Kornbluh
Carl Peterson & Lynda Sylvester
at Sylvester & Co.
Roy and *Michael*, along with all
the folks at Potter

I've been eating strawberries and blackberries for as far back as I can remember. In those long-ago days when I first made the acquaintance of these luscious morsels, berries were eaten only in season. The first strawberries always came from down around a town called Pontchatula, Louisiana. These mostly went into the making of strawberry shortcakes. As the weeks went by, and local farmers started selling strawberries by the flat along the road, preserves would be made and hand-cranked strawberry ice cream would be a Sunday regular. As a matter of fact, one of my fondest memories is of having this treat served with angel food cake for Sunday night supper—as the whole meal! Of course, it being Sunday we'd already had a big repast at noon after church service, so this was really just a delayed dessert. The beauty part, however, was that since the ice cream and cake were saved for the evening, our appetite had had time to revive and we could really do them justice. But how sublimely sinful an arrangement it was for us kids. Imagine—being able to sit down to nothing but dessert for supper!

As the weather got hotter the blackberries would appear. They seemed to grow everywhere. Blackberry vines like to have their roots near water, so they were often found close to bayous. The only drawback—aside

from their big thorns—was the fact that water snakes liked to retreat to the cool, damp shelter of the arching vines. It's a measure of how seductive blackberries were to me that I braved the possibility of a close encounter to pick them. Blackberries were used almost exclusively to make cobblers and jelly.

I didn't have blueberries until I came East to go to school. I'd heard of them years before, of course, mostly from an aunt who had ventured north and came back singing praises of blueberries.

Raspberries came later for me too, but when I had my house on Long Island I had a patch of raspberries that produced such an enormous crop twice a year that I'd invite my friends to come pick them so they wouldn't go to waste. However, I confess that even with this largesse, I've never made jams or jellies except for the refrigerator kind.

In this little book I've confined the type of berries featured to the big four—blackberries, blueberries, raspberries, and strawberries—as they can be had every place these days. I'll leave the less available types, such as gooseberries, for some other time.

I think you'll discover plenty here to pique your interest. In addition to the usual cakes, cobblers, pies, tarts, and such, you'll come across salsas, fresh chutneys, butters, dumplings, and suggestions for incorporating berries into meat dishes and salads. There is even a refreshing face mask made with strawberries. However, I didn't include berry soups because I've never really gotten their message.

Anyway, whoever said "You're the berries!" sure knew how to give a person a compliment.

Recipes

OVERLEAF: *Summer Pudding with a mountain of whipped cream.*

SUMMER PUDDING

———◆———

Summer puddings have been a staple of the British diet for generations. For some reason they have never been popular here, and it's a pity. Give this a try.

> **2¼ pounds mixed berries**
> **Grated peel of 1 lemon**
> **½ cup plus 1 tablespoon sugar**
> **5 or more slices white bread, crusts trimmed**
> **Whipped cream flavored with vanilla**

Pick over berries; cut strawberries in half if you are using them. Combine fruit with the lemon peel and sugar in a small nonreactive saucepan. Cover and simmer for 10 minutes. Take care that this doesn't boil over.

Cut each slice of bread into 3 strips and line the bottom and sides of a 4-cup soufflé dish (patching with pieces of bread if necessary). Strain fruit, reserving the pulp. Pour several tablespoons of the juice over the bottom slices of bread and let stand for a few minutes.

Fill the soufflé dish almost to the top with the fruit pulp, then pour in enough juice to moisten. Cover top with a layer of bread and dampen with a little juice. Refrigerate balance of the juice. Put a small plate, which just fits inside the dish, on top and wrap the whole thing in cling wrap. Set on a plate and weight down with a large can. Refrigerate for 24 hours.

To serve, run a knife around the edges and invert the dish onto a serving platter, being careful not to spill the accumulated juice. If juice has not stained all the bread, spoon on the reserved juice.

Serve with whipped cream and reserved juice.

Serves 4 to 6

VODKAS

◆

Berry vodkas make refreshing summer drinks on ice with club soda or tonic water. Add a twist or slice of lemon or lime. You can also put them in the freezer to be drunk neat. These are not for the amateur.

Fill a glass bottle about two-thirds full with raspberries, blueberries, blackberries, or sliced strawberries. Pour vodka over them, filling the bottle all the way. Cap it and refrigerate for several days before using.

DUMPLINGS

◆

Some people love dumplings while others can take 'em or leave 'em. I think the problem for those who don't like them is that they have had dumplings that weren't cooked properly or were handled too much in the preparation, which makes them tough. To ensure they are cooked properly, I poach my berry dumplings separately from what they are served with—in a poaching liquid that's a combination of apple juice and chicken stock.

I like berry dumplings with spicy mixtures of stewed meats, such as pork and sausages, or in chili-flavored vegetable stews. They lend a light touch to such rich dishes.

Although I've tried using other types of berries, I think blueberries are the best.

> **2 cups chicken stock**
> **2 cups unsweetened apple juice**
> **1 cup all-purpose flour**
> **1½ teaspoons baking powder**
> **½ teaspoon salt**
> **¼ teaspoon baking soda**
> **Pinch of grated nutmeg**
> **1 large egg, lightly beaten**
> **2 tablespoons butter or margarine, melted**
> **⅔ cup buttermilk**
> **½ cup blueberries, roughly pureed**

Combine stock and apple juice in a wide pot and put on to heat. Meanwhile, sift dry ingredients together into a bowl. Mix the egg, butter or margarine, and buttermilk. Pour this into the dry ingredients all at once and mix quickly. Add the blueberry puree and mix it in with a few strokes.

With the stock at a rolling boil, drop dumpling dough by the scant tablespoon into the liquid; do not crowd. Carefully turn the dumplings over with a fork after about 10 minutes. Cook until puffed and cooked through, about 15 minutes. Remove with a slotted spoon.

Serves 6

Blueberry Dumplings with a favorite pork stew.

CAKES, COBBLERS, AND CRUMBLES

I start this section with shortcake. The classic, which everyone knows, is made with strawberries; but other berries or berries combined with sliced peaches make terrific shortcakes, too. So experiment. I've given you two biscuit recipes, including the simple one my grandmother always made, which is the one I use. There is also a delightful variation using a warm cream sauce instead of the more usual whipped cream.

Next is a slightly crazy strawberry cake that's deliciously messy—in much the same way an English trifle is a delicious mess of a dessert. I suppose it could be made with other berries, but I've never had the nerve to try.

Following is something called Blueberry Buckle, a New England specialty, that is a cross between a cake and a crumble because of its topping. Then there is one of my all-time favorites, Blackberry Cobbler. You might use other berries here, but blackberry is still tops with me.

And finally there is an interesting sort of crumble called Blueberry Brown Betty.

SHORTCAKE BISCUITS I

——◆——

Butter these lightly when you split them.

>*2 cups all-purpose flour*
>*2½ teaspoons baking powder*
>*1 teaspoon salt*
>*6 tablespoons chilled unsalted butter, cut into*
>   *small pieces*
>*¾ cup milk*

Preheat the oven to 450 degrees.

Mix the dry ingredients in a bowl and cut in the chilled butter with 2 knives or a pastry blender until mixture has a coarse texture. Stir in milk all at once, mixing quickly and well. Turn out onto a floured surface and knead briefly. Cut into eight 3-inch rounds and place on an ungreased baking sheet. Bake until golden, about 13 to 15 minutes.

Makes 8 biscuits

SHORTCAKE BISCUITS II

——◆——

>*2 cups all-purpose flour*
>*2 tablespoons sugar*
>*¼ teaspoon salt*
>*4 teaspoons baking powder*
>*2 large eggs, lightly beaten*
>*4 tablespoons unsalted chilled butter, cut into*
>   *small pieces*
>*⅓ to ½ cup heavy cream*

Preheat the oven to 400 degrees.

Mix the dry ingredients quickly. Stir in the eggs. Cut in the butter, then mix in enough cream to make a dry dough. Roll out until ½ inch thick on a floured surface and cut into 8 biscuits. Place on an ungreased baking sheet and bake until golden, about 12 to 14 minutes.

Makes 8 biscuits

BERRY SHORTCAKES

Use one of the biscuit recipes above.

> **4 to 6 cups berries**
> **2 tablespoons sugar, or to taste**
> **1 cup heavy cream**
> **Vanilla, bourbon, or rum to taste**
> **8 Shortcake Biscuits I or II (opposite)**

Mash about 1 cup of the berries. Set aside a few whole berries for a garnish, then toss mashed berries with remaining whole berries and sugar. Cover and set aside in the refrigerator until they give up some of their juice, at least an hour.

Lightly whip the cream, taking care not to overwhip; it should fall easily from the spoon. Sweeten if you like and flavor it with vanilla, bourbon, or rum.

To serve, split the biscuits, place on individual plates, and put a dollop of whipped cream on the bottom half of each. Top this with the berries and their juice, and add the top halves of the biscuits. These may be topped with more whipped cream if you like, then garnish with whole berries.

Serves 8

WARM CREAM SHORTCAKES

Here is the warm version of the classic shortcake. You heat the biscuits and, instead of whipped cream, you substitute the cream sauce that follows. Inspiration for this came from Sally Schmidt of the French Laundry Restaurant in Yountville, California.

> *4 tablespoons unsalted butter*
> *¼ cup sugar*
> *2 cups heavy cream*
> *4 to 6 cups berries*

Combine the ingredients in a heavy, deep pot and bring to a boil over medium heat. This will bubble up (which is why you need the deep pot). When it does, whisk the cream down. Let it bubble up at least once more, then simmer it very gently over very low heat until thickened, about 10 minutes. If the cream gets too thick it may be thinned with a little additional cream. This may be done in advance, then reheated.

To serve, place half a split biscuit on an individual plate. Spoon on some berries and add the top half of the biscuit. Pour the warm cream over all.

Makes enough for 6 to 8 servings

STRAWBERRY CAKE

◆

Garnish this with a few fresh berries and serve it with whipped cream, if you like.

> *3 cups hulled and halved strawberries*
> *1½ cups sugar*
> *1 tablespoon unsalted butter, melted*
> *1 teaspoon vanilla extract*
> *4 large eggs, separated*
> *Pinch of salt*
> *1 teaspoon cream of tartar*
> *1 cup sifted all-purpose flour*
> *½ recipe for strawberry Refrigerator Preserves*
> *   (page 62)*
> *Whole strawberries, for garnish (optional)*

Preheat the oven to 325 degrees.

Very generously butter an 8-inch springform pan. Put the berries in the pan and sprinkle with ½ cup sugar. Set aside.

Beat the melted butter and vanilla into the egg yolks and set aside. Beat the egg whites with the salt; when they are foamy, sprinkle with cream of tartar and continue beating until stiff. Fold in the remaining sugar a little at a time. Fold in the yolk mixture. Last, fold in the flour, ¼ cup at a time. Pour over berries.

Place pan on a baking sheet and bake for 50 to 60 minutes, or until a cake tester comes out clean. Careful: This cake can seem quite done on the outside and be unbaked underneath.

Let cool for a few minutes. Place on a serving dish with a lip, then loosen around the edges and remove the outer ring. This will release quite a bit of juice. Spoon some juice over the top and then spoon preserves over the top, letting them run down the sides. Serve cake without trying to remove the bottom of the pan.

Serves 8 to 12

OVERLEAF: ***Strawberry Cake.***

BLUEBERRY BUCKLE

◆

This might be served with ice cream, Quick Berry Sauce (page 68), or spiked whipped cream.

CAKE

2 cups plus 2 tablespoons all-purpose flour
2 teaspoons baking powder
½ teaspoon salt
4 tablespoons unsalted butter, softened
¾ cup sugar
1 large egg
½ cup milk
1 pint blueberries

TOPPING

4 tablespoons unsalted butter, softened
½ cup sugar
⅓ cup sifted all-purpose flour
½ teaspoon cinnamon

Preheat the oven to 375 degrees. Grease an 8-inch springform pan.

Make the cake: Sift together the 2 cups flour, baking powder, and salt. Set aside. Cream the butter and sugar until light and fluffy. Beat in the egg. Add the flour mixture in 3 parts, alternating with the milk. Toss the berries with the remaining flour and fold them into the batter. Pour the batter into the pan and set aside.

Make the topping: Combine the topping ingredients with a fork to make a crumbly mixture. Sprinkle this over the batter, spreading it with your fingers if you like.

Bake 1 hour and test for doneness with a cake tester. If tester does not come out clean, bake an additional 5 to 10 minutes.

Allow to cool, then run a knife around the edges before removing outer ring.

Serves 6 to 8

BLACKBERRY COBBLER

——◆——

Serve this with whipped cream or ice cream.

> *1½ cups all-purpose flour*
> *Scant ¼ teaspoon salt*
> *5 tablespoons unsalted butter, frozen*
> *4 tablespoons solid vegetable shortening,*
> *   frozen*
> *4 to 5 tablespoons ice water*
> *6 to 7 cups blackberries, washed and picked*
> *¾ cup sugar*
> *4 tablespoons unsalted butter, cut into 12*
> *   pieces*
> *Additional sugar or crushed sugar cubes*

Preheat the oven to 425 degrees.

Prepare the dough by placing the flour and salt in a food processor. Add the frozen butter and vegetable shortening. Pulse until mixture is coarse. Add water and pulse until mixture holds together. Gather into a ball and put between 2 sheets of waxed paper. Flatten the ball of dough and refrigerate for about 20 minutes.

Roll out the dough on a floured surface to a ragged circle about 15 inches in diameter. Roll onto the rolling pin windowshade fashion, then unroll over a 9-inch round ovenproof dish 2 or more inches deep. Allow excess to drape over the sides. Mound the berries in the dish, sprinkle with the sugar, and dot with the butter. Flop the edges on top of the berries, using any pieces that may have broken off to patch. Sprinkle with a little additional sugar or crushed sugar cubes. Bake until golden and bubbly, about 45 minutes.

Serves 6

BLUEBERRY BROWN BETTY

———◆———

Serve with ice cream or whipped cream.

6 cups blueberries, washed and picked over
½ cup firmly packed light brown sugar
½ teaspoon ground cinnamon
Grated rind and juice of ½ large lemon
2 heaping cups large, very coarse fresh bread
 crumbs (see Note)
⅓ cup unsalted butter, melted

Preheat the oven to 350 degrees. Butter a deep 7 by 9-inch ovenproof dish.

Toss together the berries, brown sugar, cinnamon, and lemon rind and juice. Place half the berries in the prepared dish. Toss half the bread crumbs with half the melted butter. Spread the crumbs over the berries. Top with the remaining berries and then the last of the crumbs and butter as above.

Bake for 30 minutes, then cover lightly with foil and bake another 15 minutes or until berries are bubbling.

Serves 6 to 8

Note: Cut crusts off slices of dense white bread and tear into large pieces. Place in a processor and pulse just enough to make large, soft bread crumbs.

Some of my friends like these chutneys and salsas so much they eat them like salad. Whatever your preference, they are a terrific addition to any meat dish and are especially good with the sort you cook on the grill in the summer.

When you use strawberries here, cut them into large chunks; leave other berries whole.

FRESH BERRY CHUTNEY

Allow to marinate for about an hour before serving.

> *²/₃ cup golden raisins*
> *¹/₂ cup fresh orange juice*
> *2 cups berries*
> *5 green onions, minced, with some green*
> *1 garlic clove, minced*
> *1 small red chili pepper (about 4 inches),*
>   *seeded and minced*
> *1¹/₂ tablespoons minced fresh ginger*
> *3 tablespoons minced cilantro*
> *1 to 1¹/₂ tablespoons fresh lime juice*
> *Salt*

Put the raisins in a small nonreactive bowl and cover with the orange juice. Allow to sit for about 30 minutes. Drain, reserving the raisins and discarding the juice.

Toss the raisins with the remaining ingredients, mixing well.
Makes about 2¹/₂ cups

FRESH BERRY SALSA

This is especially good with sliced strawberries.

> **2 cups diced ripe tomatoes**
> **½ cup diced yellow bell pepper**
> **1 cup berries**
> **3 tablespoons seeded and minced jalapeño
>   pepper**
> **½ cup diced white onion**
> **3 tablespoons minced cilantro**
> **1 teaspoon salt**
> **3 tablespoons balsamic vinegar**

Mix all the ingredients in a bowl and refrigerate, covered, for 1 hour. Allow to come back to room temperature before serving.
   Makes about 3 cups

You can make berry vinegar using rasp-berries, blackberries, or blueberries. Strawberries don't work too well with my simple method; their flavor doesn't seem quite potent enough.

I find these sweet-tart vinegars have lots of uses—for instance, in vinaigrette to dress salads containing strong, pep-pery, or slightly bitter combinations of greens. Or for piquing sauces and gravies. They can do wonders added to chicken gravy (simmer it down a bit after adding) or sprinkled over grilled vegetables.

To make the vinegar, boil any small glass container in water for a few min-utes, dry it, and fill with one kind of berries. Pour enough apple cider vine-gar over the berries to cover them. Cap the container, and place it in a spot where the sun will heat it every day. Let the vinegar mature for 8 days, then strain the liquid by pouring it through a sieve into another sterilized bottle with a cap. Discard the berries.

CHEESE AND FRUIT SALAD

———◆———

I think you'll find this combination of berries and cheese a surprising and refreshing first course.

DRESSING

2 tablespoons raspberry vinegar
7 tablespoons olive oil
½ teaspoon black pepper
3 tablespoons Creole mustard

ASSEMBLY

1¼ cups raspberries
1¼ cups blueberries
6 ounces Gouda, grated
6 ounces Jack cheese, grated
18 leaves Boston lettuce, cleaned and dried

Make the dressing: Whisk all ingredients together, or shake them in a covered jar, until well combined.

Assemble the salad: Combine the berries in a bowl and toss with about 3 tablespoons of the dressing. In another bowl, combine the cheeses and toss with the remaining dressing. Arrange 3 lettuce leaves on 6 salad plates and top with a good dollop of the cheese mixture. Sprinkle with the dressed berries.

Serves 6

ENDIVE CARROT SALAD WITH BERRY VINAIGRETTE

6 large heads Belgian endive, leaves separated, washed, and dried
2 carrots, scraped and cut into very thin strips with a vegetable peeler
¾ teaspoon salt
½ teaspoon black pepper
2 tablespoons berry vinegar
6 tablespoons canola oil
3 tablespoons olive oil
¼ cup fresh berries

Arrange endive leaves on individual and salad plates and sprinkle carrot strips over the center of each. Whisk together the remaining ingredients for the vinaigrette except the berries. Just before spooning over the endive, mash in the berries. Grind more pepper over each salad if you like.

Serves 6

KITCHEN COSMETICS

I have two friends, Steve Byckiewicz and Bob MacLeod, who own a company called Kiss My Face, which specializes in beauty and health products. When I mentioned this book to them, Steve mysteriously said "I might have something for you."

True to his word, several days later I received a page from Jeanne Rose's Kitchen Cosmetics, *which suggested that "an excellent mask for tired skin is to mash some fresh strawberries and mix them with yogurt and a bit of almond meal to hold it together. Apply this to your skin and lie down for 1½ hours. You will get up with your skin feeling much more refreshed and revitalized. Then simply rinse off the mask with clear water."*

Why not?

Berry fritters can be served as part of the main meal, especially with ham or lamb. They may also be served as dessert, sprinkled with confectioners' sugar.

Of course, the pancakes make a great late Sunday breakfast. And I suspect you can find some way to use the muffins.

MUFFINS

If you use strawberries here, select medium ones and cut them in half. They'll give off a good bit of liquid as they cook, so the muffins will not rise as high as blueberry muffins, but they still taste mighty good.

> *2 cups plus 3 tablespoons all-purpose flour*
> *½ teaspoon salt*
> *4 teaspoons baking powder*
> *½ teaspoon ground cinnamon*
> *½ cup plus 2 tablespoons sugar*
> *2 large eggs, well beaten*
> *6 tablespoons unsalted butter, melted*
> *⅔ cup milk*
> *2½ cups blueberries, blackberries, raspberries,*
>   *or strawberries*

Preheat the oven to 425 degrees. Using a 12-cup and a 6-cup muffin tin, either grease the tins or place 16 paper cups in the tins. Set aside.

Sift together 2 cups flour, the salt, baking powder, and cinnamon. Set aside.

Beat together the sugar and eggs, then add the butter and milk. Briefly stir into the dry ingredients; do not overmix. Sprinkle the remaining flour over the berries and toss to coat. Fold these into the batter. Fill the muffin cups two-thirds full. Bake 20 to 25 minutes, or until a tester comes out clean.

Makes 16 muffins

PANCAKES

———◆———

I think I like raspberries the best for pancakes.

> **1 cup self-rising cake flour**
> **2 teaspoons sugar**
> **¼ teaspoon baking soda**
> **¼ teaspoon salt**
> **1 large egg, lightly beaten**
> **1 cup buttermilk**
> **1 to 2 tablespoons unsalted butter, melted**
> **1 cup raspberries**

Have a griddle well oiled with vegetable oil and hot.

Sift together the dry ingredients. Combine the egg, buttermilk, and butter in a small bowl, mixing well. Quickly stir into dry ingredients; do not overmix. Sprinkle the berries on top and fold in gently.

Place on the griddle by large spoonfuls. Cook until golden on the underside, about 2 to 3 minutes, then turn. Cook another minute or so until done.

Makes 12 or more 3-inch pancakes

OVERLEAF: *Raspberry Pancakes garnished with sliced strawberries.*

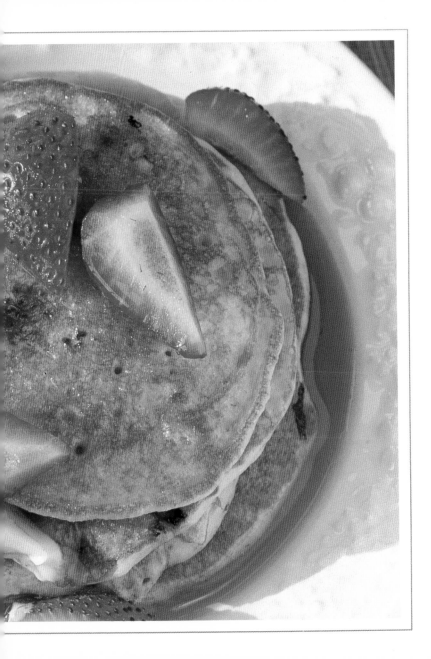

RASPBERRY FRITTERS

If you use blackberries to make the fritters, just follow the instructions. If you use blueberries, stir them into the batter all at once. Strawberries don't work very well here.

> *1½ cups all-purpose flour*
> *2 rounded teaspoons baking powder*
> *½ teaspoon salt*
> *1 tablespoon granulated sugar*
> *2 tablespoons unsalted butter, melted*
> *2 large eggs, lightly beaten*
> *Milk*
> *1 cup lightly sugared raspberries*
> *Oil for frying*
> *Confectioners' sugar and/or berry syrup*
> *(page 72)*

Mix the dry ingredients in a bowl. Make a well in the center and pour in the butter and eggs. Blend well. Add milk a tablespoon at a time, stirring after each addition until you have a batter that's smooth but not runny. You should only just be able to shake the batter off the spoon. Don't mix the berries in.

Heat the oil in a deep pot (you should have at least 2 inches of oil) until very hot, about 365 degrees. Stir some batter into a quarter of the berries. Drop by tablespoons into the hot oil and fry until golden. Be careful not to burn them. Fritters can deceive you, looking done on the outside while remaining uncooked inside, so try one or two until you get it right. Fry the fritters in batches, until all batter and berries are used.

Sprinkle with confectioners' sugar or drizzle on a bit of berry syrup.

Makes about 12 fritters

HOT AND COLD SOUFFLES

Hot berry soufflés fall into that category of desserts I choose on those occasions when I want to make something just for the fun of it. Since they have to be prepared and baked to be served after the main part of the dinner, they are difficult to manage if you are not working with a helper who can get them started while guests are dining. But they are *worth the trouble now and again.*

On the other hand, cold berry soufflés are a snap to make in advance and are delicious, if a bit more calorie intensive.

HOT BERRY SOUFFLÉ

⸻◆⸻

This is based on James Beard's simple basic recipe. Use the same type of jam as fresh berries here.

> *Granulated sugar*
> *6 large egg whites*
> *¼ teaspoon salt*
> *¼ teaspoon cream of tartar*
> *⅓ cup sugar*
> *2 tablespoons jam*
> *1 tablespoon raspberry* **eau-de-vie**
> *2 cups pureed berries*

Preheat the oven to 400 degrees.

Generously butter a 2-quart soufflé dish and dust it with granulated sugar. Set aside.

Beat the egg whites until foamy and sprinkle with the salt and cream of tartar. Continue beating; when soft peaks are formed, sprinkle with the sugar in several batches and beat to stiff peaks.

Mix the jam and eau-de-vie into the berry puree. Fold gently into the egg whites.

Pour into the prepared soufflé dish and bake until puffy and golden, about 25 to 30 minutes. To test for doneness, insert a cake tester into the side of the soufflé (not the top). Tester should come out clean but wet.

Serves 6

COLD BERRY SOUFFLÉ

6 large eggs, separated, at room temperature
½ cup granulated sugar
1 tablespoon unflavored gelatin
1 cup pureed berries
1 tablespoon kirsch
1 cup heavy cream
¼ cup confectioners' sugar
¼ cup cream of tartar
¼ teaspoon salt

Put an oiled waxed-paper collar around a 6-cup soufflé dish. (If you don't want to bother with a collar, use a slightly larger dish.)

Place the yolks, granulated sugar, and gelatin in a bowl and beat until light and thick. Put mixture in the top of a double boiler and stir in the berry puree. Cook over barely boiling water just long enough to dissolve the sugar and gelatin, several minutes, then set aside to cool.

Stir the kirsch into the egg-raspberry mixture. Whip the cream, adding confectioners' sugar 1 tablespoon at a time until stiff. Fold the cream into the raspberry mixture.

Beat the egg whites until foamy. Add the cream of tartar and salt, and continue to beat until soft peaks form. Fold the whites into the berry mixture and pour into the prepared soufflé dish. Refrigerate for several hours or until set.

Serve the soufflé topped with additional berries and Quick Berry Sauce (page 68), if desired.

Serves 6 to 8

Strawberries are best when used in pies and tarts if they are either left uncooked or combined with reduced berries. The same is true to a lesser degree of raspberries. Here are some versions of each that I like. Lots of good stuff here!

BLUEBERRY PIE

PASTRY

2¼ cups sifted whole wheat flour
¼ cup sugar
½ teaspoon salt
**½ cup solid vegetable shortening, frozen and
    cut into bits**
1 teaspoon distilled white vinegar
About 6 tablespoons ice water

FILLING

½ cup all-purpose flour
⅔ cup sugar
2 teaspoons finely grated lemon zest
**6 cups fresh blueberries, washed and picked
    over**
2 tablespoons fresh lemon juice
**4 tablespoons unsalted butter, cut into 12 or
    more pieces**

Make the pastry: Combine the whole wheat flour, sugar, and salt in the bowl of a food processor. Sprinkle the shortening on top and pulse several times until the mixture is coarse. With the motor running, add the vinegar and 2 tablespoons of the water. Process briefly, add another tablespoon of water and pulse. Keep adding water a tablespoon at a time until dough forms a mass.

Divide the dough in half, one part slightly larger than the other. Place each ball between 2 sheets of waxed paper and flatten slightly. Wrap and refrigerate for about 1 hour.

Preheat the oven to 400 degrees.

Make the filling: Combine the flour, sugar, and zest for the filling. Add the berries and toss to coat. Toss in lemon juice and set aside.

Roll out the larger ball of dough into a circle about 13 inches in diameter. Line a 10-inch pie pan, and trim edges leaving about a 1-inch overhang.

Mound the filling in the shell and dot with the butter.

Roll out the second ball into a 12-inch circle and place over filling. Trim edges. Fold over lower crust and trim edges. Cut in several steam slits. You could also cut the top crust into strips and make a lattice top.

Place on a foil-covered baking sheet (this might bubble over slightly) in the center of the oven and bake for 20 minutes. Reduce heat to 350 degrees and bake an additional 25 minutes, or until lightly browned. Let cool to room temperature on a rack before serving.

Serves 6 to 8

STRAWBERRY PIE

Incidentally, this adapts well to individual pies.

PASTRY

1½ cups all-purpose flour
¾ teaspoon salt
2 tablespoons sugar
5 tablespoons ice water
¼ cup solid vegetable shortening, chilled and
cut into bits
2 tablespoons unsalted butter, chilled and cut
into bits

FILLING

Approximately 1½ quarts strawberries
1 cup sugar
3 tablespoons cornstarch
½ cup water
1 tablespoon unsalted butter
1 cup heavy cream, whipped and flavored with
vanilla extract

Make the pastry: Sift together the flour, salt, and sugar. Remove
⅓ cup of this and mix with the ice water to make a paste. Set
aside.

Place the remaining flour mixture in a food processor and
add shortening and butter. Process until coarse. Scrape in the
paste and process until mixture forms a ball. Place ball between 2 sheets of waxed paper and flatten slightly. Refrigerate
for about 30 minutes.

Preheat the oven to 425 degrees.

Roll out the dough on a lightly floured surface into a 14-inch circle. Line a 9-inch pie pan with the dough, allowing excess to hang over the sides. Trim, leaving about ½ inch all around. Fold edges under and crimp. Place a sheet of foil on top of the pastry and weight it down with dried beans. Bake 5 to 7 minutes, or until golden. Carefully loosen the edges. When almost cool, slide shell off onto a serving plate.

Make the filling: Mash enough berries to fill a cup. Halve the remaining berries, saving a few perfect ones for garnish.

Combine the mashed berries, sugar, cornstarch, and water in a small saucepan and cook over medium heat, stirring constantly, until mixture comes to a boil. Continue cooking for about 2 minutes over low heat until the mixture is thickened and clear. Stir in the butter and cook until melted, then allow to cool slightly.

Place the halved berries in the baked crust and pour the cooked ones over them. Shake the serving plate gently so the glaze seeps down and around the uncooked berries.

Chill for several hours, then serve topped with the flavored whipped cream and garnished with the whole berries.

Serves 6 to 8

OVERLEAF: ***Strawberry Pie.***

DEEP-DISH BLACKBERRY PIE

———◆———

PASTRY

2 cups all-purpose flour
¼ teaspoon salt
1 teaspoon sugar
¾ cup unsalted butter, chilled and cut into bits
5 tablespoons ice water

FILLING

5 cups blackberries, washed
1 cup plus 1 tablespoon sugar
2 tablespoons all-purpose flour
4 tablespoons unsalted butter, cut into bits
1 tablespoon fresh lemon juice
½ teaspoon ground cinnamon

Make the pastry: Place the dry ingredients in a food processor. Add the butter and process until mixture has a coarse texture. With the machine running, add water a tablespoon at a time until dough holds together. Gather dough into a ball and wrap in waxed paper. Refrigerate for 30 minutes.

Preheat the oven to 425 degrees.

Roll out half the dough on a lightly floured surface. Line an 8-inch deep-dish pie pan, leaving about ½ inch all around.

Make the filling: Place the berries in a bowl. Mix 1 cup of sugar with the flour and sprinkle over the berries. Sprinkle the chilled butter pieces and lemon juice over all and toss together. Mound into the lined pie pan.

Roll out the other portion of dough and place it over the top. Cut it to fit and bring the extra half-inch around the outside of the bottom crust up over the top crust and seal. Crimp; cut steam slits in the top. Mix the remaining tablespoon of sugar with the cinnamon and sprinkle it over the top. Bake until crust is dark golden, about 35 to 40 minutes.

Serves 6 to 8

BLUEBERRY TART

———◆———

1 cup all-purpose flour
⅓ cup confectioners' sugar
½ cup unsalted butter, softened
2 tablespoons granulated sugar
1 large egg
¾ cup sour cream
1 pint large blueberries
4 teaspoons fresh lemon juice
½ cup red currant jelly

Preheat the oven to 350 degrees.

Place the flour, confectioners' sugar, and butter in a mixing bowl and, using your fingers, work it to form a stiff dough. Press and pat into the bottom of a 4¼ by 14-inch tart pan with a removable bottom. It is not necessary to line the sides.

Mix the granulated sugar, egg, and sour cream and spread over the dough. Arrange blueberries in a single layer over the sour cream mixture. Sprinkle with the lemon juice.

Bake until the dough is done, about 50 minutes.

Let the tart cool for about 10 minutes, then loosen around the edges and slide off onto a rectangular plate. Heat the jelly and brush it over all and smooth evenly.

Serves 6 to 8

RASPBERRY JAM TART

———◆———

Serve with a little flavored cream or ice cream.

1 cup all-purpose flour
¼ cup sugar
½ teaspoon baking powder
Pinch of salt
*4 tablespoons unsalted butter, chilled and cut
    into small pieces*
1 large egg, lightly beaten

6 very generous tablespoons raspberry jam
3 large eggs, separated
5 tablespoons sugar
Salt
6 tablespoons unsalted butter, melted
6 tablespoons soft white bread crumbs
6 tablespoons coarsely ground walnuts

Make the pastry: Place the flour, sugar, baking powder, and salt in a processor and pulse a few times to mix. Add butter and pulse until coarse. Add egg and pulse until mixture holds together. Gather into a ball and place between 2 sheets of waxed paper, flatten slightly, and wrap. Refrigerate for 30 minutes.

Preheat the oven to 375 degrees.

Roll out the pastry and line the bottom of a 9-inch loose-bottom tart pan, coming about halfway up the insides. Mend any areas that may have broken loose in the process.

Make the filling: Spread the jam evenly over the pastry. Beat together the egg yolks, sugar, a pinch of salt, and the melted butter. Stir in the bread crumbs and nuts. Beat the egg whites until they are stiff and fold into the yolk-nut mixture. Spread this evenly over the jam and bake for 30 to 35 minutes, or until filling has risen and turned lightly golden. When cooled, loosen edges and slide off onto a serving plate.

Serves 6 to 8

BERRY AND JAM HAND TARTS

*1 recipe for pastry from Strawberry Pie
   (page 52)*
1 tablespoon unsalted butter, melted
½ cup soft bread crumbs
*1 cup strawberry Refrigerator Preserves
   (page 62)*
12 medium strawberries

Preheat the oven to 350 degrees.

Roll out half the dough into a thin sheet. In a bowl, mix the butter and bread crumbs, then the preserves. If you have a tart maker (see Note), heap a tablespoon of the jam-crumb mixture in the center of a 5-inch square of rolled-out dough. Top with a berry or two. Place another square of pastry on top, cut, and seal with tart maker. Remove to a lightly greased baking sheet. When first sheet of dough is finished, repeat with the second.

If you don't have a tart maker, use the same square, but put the filling to one side and fold the dough over onto itself, making a filled triangle. Dampen the dough where the top and bottom parts meet, and seal by pressing the 2 open sides together with the tines of a fork.

Bake until golden, about 20 to 25 minutes. Cool on a rack.
Makes 8 tarts

Note: You can order a tart maker from Kitchen Connection, Inc., 8405 W. 45th Street, Lyons, IL 60534 (telephone: 708-442-5232). They are called Tart Masters and come in several shapes and sizes.

The recipes for blueberries, raspberries, blackberries, and strawberries are mostly the same. The only difference is the amount of sugar used, which may vary with the tartness of the berries. Blackberries are especially tart and will need the most sugar.

REFRIGERATOR PRESERVES

This jam is not too sweet. Simply add more sugar to another batch if you like your jam sweeter. You may also add a little commercial pectin if you like; follow package directions.

> **1 quart berries**
> **1 to 1½ cups sugar**
> **1 teaspoon fresh lemon juice**

Wash and hull the berries. If using strawberries, quarter them. In a small enamel pot, alternate layers of berries and sugar. Bring to a boil, stirring from time to time, and then turn heat down. Add lemon juice and simmer for 8 to 10 minutes, stirring often.

With a slotted spoon, remove fruit to a small jar. Continue simmering juice until it is reduced by half and syrupy. Pour over berries. Allow to cool. Cover and keep refrigerated.

Makes almost 1 pint

BERRY WALNUT CONSERVE

1 12-ounce package frozen berries
½ cup sugar
1 tablespoon fresh lemon juice
2 tablespoons vodka
1½ cups coarsely chopped walnuts
¼ teaspoon ground cinnamon

Combine the berries, sugar, lemon juice, and vodka in the top of a double boiler. Stir and cook over low heat for 20 minutes or until thickened. Mix in walnuts and cinnamon. Allow to cool and store, covered, in the refrigerator.

Makes about 2 cups

OVERLEAF: *Strawberry Refrigerator Preserves.*

I think you'll find lots of uses for these recipes. The sauces can be toppings for poached fruit, ice cream, flans, and other custards. There are also berry sauces that are especially tasty with meat.

The syrups can be used on many desserts as well as on cakes, pancakes, and fruit. The same for the honeys.

Berry butters are a fine accompaniment to breakfast biscuits or toast, and also may be used on pancakes and muffins.

BERRY CARAMEL SAUCE

1 pint berries
½ cup water
1½ cups sugar
½ cup Sauternes
1 tablespoon fresh lemon juice
Kirsch to taste (optional)

Puree the berries and strain to remove seeds or skins. Measure 1 cup puree. Set aside.

Place ¼ cup of water and the sugar in a heavy saucepan. Let stand until sugar is moist through. Cook over medium-high heat until sugar is light golden in color, stirring constantly. Sugar will begin to caramelize. Remove from heat and set the pan in the sink. Carefully (it will spit), stir in the remaining water. Return pan to stove and add wine. Cook over medium heat, stirring constantly, until caramel has completely dissolved. Remove from heat and add the puree a tablespoon at a time. Add lemon juice and a few drops of kirsch if desired. Store in the refrigerator.

Makes about 1½ cups

QUICK BERRY SAUCE

1 pint washed berries
Sugar or artificial sweetener
Lemon juice
Kirsch (optional)

Place berries in a blender or food processor with several tablespoons sugar or sweetener. Puree and taste for sweetness. Add more if necessary. Add a teaspoon of lemon juice and taste again, adding more juice if you like. Do the same with kirsch if you are using it.

Strain out the seeds and refrigerate until ready to use.

Makes about 1 cup

OPPOSITE: *Quick Blackberry Sauce.*

BERRY SAUCE FOR MEAT I

Here is a sauce that you can use with pork chops or anything else cooked in a skillet so you can use the sauce to deglaze the pan.

> *2 cups chicken stock*
> *1 tablespoon blackberry or raspberry vinegar*
> *   (page 35)*
> *1 tablespoon butter*
> *1 generous cup fresh blackberries or*
> *   raspberries*
> *Salt and pepper*

Deglaze the pan with 2 cups of stock, then simmer for a minute or two. Add the vinegar and whip in the butter. Add the berries and mash them gently. Reduce until slightly thickened. Correct seasoning. Spoon the sauce over the chops as they are served and garnish with a few fresh berries if desired.

Makes enough for 6 servings of meat

BERRY SAUCE FOR MEAT II

———◆———

This is especially good with crisp duck.

>*1 cup blackberries or raspberries*
>*1 cup Port wine*
>*3½ cups chicken stock, reduced to 2½ cups*
>*1 teaspoon salt or to taste*
>*½ teaspoon white pepper (optional)*

Bring the berries and wine to a boil in a nonreactive saucepan over high heat. Continue at a rolling boil until reduced by half, 10 to 12 minutes. Add the stock and bring to a boil again. Strain, season, and serve with heated fowl.

Makes enough for 6 servings of meat

BERRY SYRUP

1 pint berries
1½ cups sugar
2 teaspoons fresh lemon juice

Put the berries in a small enamel pan and top with the sugar. Place over low heat, stirring occasionally. When bubbly, cook for about 10 minutes. Add lemon juice. Let cool slightly, then push through a sieve to remove seeds and/or skin. Pour into a container, cover tightly, and store in the refrigerator.

Makes about 1½ cups

BERRY HONEY

It's really better to use frozen berries for this because they are usually cheaper and the flavor is all that counts.

1 generous cup frozen berries
1½ cups honey
¼ cup water
1 teaspoon or more grated lemon rind
(optional)

Combine the berries, ½ cup honey, and water in a small saucepan. Simmer slowly over low heat for about 15 minutes. Stir in the balance of the honey, then allow to cool. Stir in optional lemon rind. Refrigerate.

Makes about 2½ cups

OPPOSITE: *Raspberry Honey.*

BERRY AND BLACK CHERRY SAUCE

*1 17-ounce can pitted black cherries, drained,
   reserving the syrup*
2-inch strip of lemon rind
1 tablespoon fresh lemon juice
1½ tablespoons cornstarch
2 tablespoons water
1 cup berries (halved, if strawberries)

Place the cherry syrup in a medium saucepan and add the rind
and lemon juice. Set aside.

Mix the cornstarch with the water until smooth. Stir into the
syrup and cook over medium heat, stirring all the while, until
mixture is clear and thickened, about 10 minutes. Add the
cherries off the heat and allow to cool. Just before serving, mix
in the berries.

Makes about 2 cups

BERRY BUTTER

Use the same type of fresh berry as in the syrup.

12 tablespoons unsalted butter, softened
½ cup Berry Syrup (page 72)
½ cup berries, crushed

Put all ingredients in a bowl and blend thoroughly with a hand mixer at high speed. Smooth mixture into a bowl and cover. Keep refrigerated.

Makes about 1 cup

OVERLEAF: *Blackberry Butter.*

When making berry ices or ice creams, remember that freezing diminishes the sweetness, so the mixture should be a little sweeter than you might like before it is frozen. And since different types of berries, and even different batches of the same kind of berry, vary in natural sweetness, trust your own preferences when making these.

SUGARLESS BERRY ICE

2 10-ounce packages frozen berries, almost thawed

⅔ cup chilled unsweetened apple juice or ice water

2 tablespoons eau-de-vie *or fruit brandy of the berry you are using (optional)*

Puree the almost-thawed berries in a food processor or blender, strain, then stir in the apple juice.

Pour the mixture into an ice cream maker and freeze according to the manufacturer's directions until almost firm. If you are using *eau-de-vie*, add it now; if not, continue freezing until firm.

Makes about 1½ pints

BERRY ICE CREAM

6 tablespoons sugar
1½ teaspoons all-purpose flour
Pinch of salt
1 cup half-and-half
1 large egg, lightly beaten
1 cup milk
1 teaspoon vanilla extract
1 pint fresh berries, crushed

Mix sugar, flour, and salt in the top of a double boiler. Stir in the half-and-half, then cook over boiling water for about 5 minutes, stirring all the while. Cover and continue cooking over boiling water for 10 minutes more. Remove from heat and spoon a little of the hot mixture into the beaten egg to warm it. Add the warmed egg to the milk and return double boiler to the heat.

Place mixture over hot, not boiling, water and stir constantly until mixture coats spoon, about 5 minutes. Strain and chill.

When cold, stir in the milk, vanilla, and berries.

Pour the mixture into an ice cream maker and freeze according to the manufacturer's directions.

Makes about 1½ pints

SWEET SIMPLICITY

Most of us know from eating them sun-warmed right off the vine or bush that berries don't really need to be enhanced to taste sublime. But human nature being what it is, most of us can't seem to resist a little embellishing. If berries are perfect when just picked at their ripest, how about adding just a sprinkle of sugar and a little heavy cream, or whipped cream flavored with vanilla, or—better still—flavored with *eau-de-vie* made from the fruit.

In this mood of gilding the berry, so to speak, I'd like to add an inspired marriage that I first encountered in Italy years ago: sweetened small strawberries doused with fresh lemon juice. You see large glass bowls of them prepared this way sitting among the other delights on the antipasto table as you enter most trattorias. This slightly sweetened lemon bath makes the natural flavor of the berry sing. Try it.